The Toilet Tractate

Arthur Belefant, P.E.

Published by Benjamin Ross & Lane
Melbourne Beach, FL
www.benjaminrosslane.com

ISBN 978-0-9629-5557-0

CONTENTS

AUTHOR'S INTRODUCTION

Looking over my files, I find that I have been writing a column, "Gourmet's Guide," for *SCAM*, the monthly magazine for Space Coast area Mensa, for over ten years. That's more than 120 articles so far.

It all began in the summer of 1992 when I was disgruntled at our coming national elections. I wrote an essay outlining a proposed change in our voting system that would better reflect the opinions of the electorate. I did not expect that any change would come about because of my suggestion, but I felt that I needed a larger audience for my ideas than the limited number of friends to whom I could directly communicate.

I submitted my article to *SCAM* and to my delight it was published in the August 1992 issue. True to my anticipation, nothing came of my suggestion, but I was happy to have aired my position. After that issue was published, I was approached by the then-editor to write further for *SCAM*. At first I demurred, not being sure of what I could write about or how long I could do it.

After some prodding, I agreed to try if I were allowed to write about food. I was not exactly a novice to food writing. Many years ago, I was the restaurant reviewer and food columnist for the Tokyo *Asahi Evening News*. Also, I had published a book, not a cookbook but a book about international food, *The Gourmet's Guide*, which is now out of print, and two cookbooks, *A Greek Dinner* and *A Japanese Dinner*, on audio tape. After some time and many articles about food published in *SCAM*, I decided to expand my mandate to write about other subjects.

Since then, in my column I have not restricted myself too closely to the column's titled subject. I have covered in addition to food and its preparation: travel, political commentary, social customs, and other non-food subjects. All columns were related, sometimes distantly, to eating.

Occasionally I write about toilets. The subject is related to eating because it is dependent on a function of the alimentary tract, albeit the end opposite from ingestion. It can be considered a special case of Kickoff's Law, "What goes in must come out."

You may wonder about my interest in toilets, but I come by my interest honestly and it is not a prurient interest. By profession I am a mechanical/electrical engineer. The design of toilet facilities is a major part of the design of any building or facility that has human inhabitants. Thus, I am required to know much about how toilets are used, and because much of my career has been designing facilities abroad, my experience includes the use of toilets, both physical and cultural, in most parts of the world.

Much of what I have written on the subject is the result of that background. These articles about toilets are some of the best received of any articles that I have written. Not only do my readers relish the subject of toilets but also it seems to have a general popular interest.

Most of these chapters appeared as articles about toilets in *SCAM*, and some of them also appeared in the national plumbing magazine, *PM Engineering*. A few chapters have not been published elsewhere. Those articles that have been published elsewhere have been updated and modified to suit the format of this book; otherwise they are as they were published.

I occasionally teach a facilities design course at a local university. The course covers aspects of the mechanical and electrical design elements: lighting, power, communications, air-conditioning, fire protection, plumbing, and so forth. You will probably not be surprised that the subject that garners the most attention and foments the best attendance among my senior level and graduate students is toilets.

So, although there is much humor in these articles, we must keep in mind that disposal of human waste is a serious business. The aphorism of the sanitary engineering community is, "It may be shit to you but it is bread and butter to us."

This, then, is a compilation of toilet articles for your edification and enlightenment.

Arthur Belefant

Melbourne Beach, Florida

A COMPUTER MODEL OF A TOILET

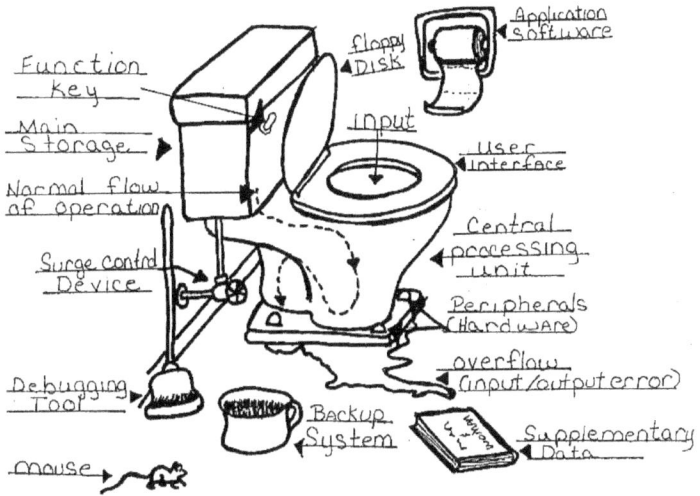

Function Key

Main Storage

Normal flow of operation

Surge control Device

Debugging Tool

mouse

floppy DISK

Application software

input

user Interface

Central processing unit

Peripherals (Hardware)

overflow (input/output error)

Backup System

Supplementary Data

Chapter 1

NAMING THE UN-NAMEABLE

In or adjacent to almost every facility designed for human inhabitation there is a private room or place set aside for performing one or two of our natural bodily functions. It is in homes, offices, shops, airplanes, and now even on busses.

This room or place has existed for thousands of years, some of the earliest known examples being in the Minoan civilization on Crete. However, there is a difficulty in naming that room. Although we all know what room we are talking about, there is no one word that clearly and unequivocally denotes it. Certain descriptive words or terms, such as "john," "men's", "lady's", "gent's", "little boy's", and "little girl's" are used to identify the room by using a gender specific word for its name.

These words and terms do not describe the function of the room, but denote the room as being specifically for use by men or women. That room is also known as a rest room, though I doubt that many people go there to rest. It is sometimes known as a powder room because ofttimes the ladies would leave the table to "powder their noses." As the ladies left, in the less couth societies, a cry would go up from the men of "We know where you're going!" They undoubtedly did, but they wouldn't put it directly into words.

"Retiring room" is another term used occasionally, although I can't see how either of the common English meanings for the word "retire" (to go to sleep at night or to cease work after reaching an advanced age) can be associated with the true function of that room.

Many of that room's common names are euphemistic terms which are based on a secondary or related function to which that room is sometimes put. For example; because we are taught to clean our hands after performing that function for which that room is provided, the room is often called a washroom, lavatory, or latrine (derived from the Latin *lavare* - to wash). Another common term for that place is "bathroom."

In a home it is true that people also do bathe in bathrooms. However, when the bathtub is omitted from the bathroom, the room is called a half-bath, an oxymoron. No doubt, this name is used because there is no good name for the other half of that room. The most common English word for that room is "toilet." The word is derived from the French word for a person's clothing or the place where one dresses, ultimately from *toilette*, "a little towel," used in cleaning one's hands or face.

A separate dressing room, especially for the ladies, was often provided adjacent to the sleeping quarters in grand French chateaux. Perhaps that's where the chamber pot was stored and used. After the decline of the Roman civilization and prior to the reintroduction of indoor plumbing in modern times, that bodily function was often performed in a small structure remote from the main house that was designed and built especially for that specific purpose. It is still the case in many areas of the U. S. and other countries where indoor plumbing is not available.

The building is aptly named an outhouse. Because the function is absolutely needed, the outhouse was sometimes referred to as the "necessary house" or the "necessary." The name stuck to that room when it was moved indoors. Of all the common bodily functions such as eating, drinking, sneezing, coughing, sweating, only that function seems to be circumscribed from public view.

Even people engaging in sexual intercourse and men urinating have been depicted in movies released for the general public. Thus, the room for that function has often been called a privy - a private place.

In public toilets, where only men would be, the urinals generally are open to view to anyone in the room, but that fixture is separately enclosed and hidden in individual stalls behind doors. The origins of the word "head" as it relates to that room supposedly goes back to the days of sailing ships.

Sailing ships had no special room for that function as all waste was simply and unceremoniously thrown overboard. To perform that function, a sailor would go to the bow or head end of the ship and climb the rigging below the bow sprit. On large sailing ships, a board with holes in it was deployed in that area.

The rigging area was the most private part aboard the ship. Someone using the "head" could not be seen by anyone on deck. Also, the splashing of the bow waves would keep that area clean and, because on a sailing ship, the wind blows from the rear to the front, odors would not waft across the deck.

I suppose that the sensibilities of other peoples are basically no different than that of Americans. In European hotels, sleeping rooms are given numbers such as 43, 76, 261, and so on with some numerical consistency between the number and the location of the room. In those hotels that have only one of those rooms for each floor or building, that unmentionable room is marked by the empty number 00 regardless of where it is located. Often that room has no other designation. A room labeled "bathroom" generally has nothing but a tub in it.

The places for that function on the island of Jamaica are called "Public Conveniences." Accessible to the public they are, being found in parks and squares, but unfortunately they are not convenient, as all that I saw were locked shut.

Another designation used all over Europe and most of the rest of the world is "WC." This is despite the fact that there is no "W" in many European languages and that the letters mean nothing except in English. But to Germans, Italians, Spaniards, and for that matter, even Greeks who do not use the Roman alphabet, the meaning of "WC" is unequivocal. "WC" is the abbreviation for the English term "water closet."

In most of the non-English speaking world, a WC is the room in which that fixture is located. The use of the abbreviation of the English "water closet" in non-English speaking countries is no stranger than the common British usage of the word "loo," from the French "l'eau," meaning "water," for the same room.

But what exactly is a "water closet?" To Europeans a WC is the room in which that fixture is located. To American engineers, builders, and suppliers, "water closet" designates the fixture on which you sit when you are using that room, not the room.

Originally, "water closet" referred specifically to the tank or cistern that held the flushing water, so that calling that fixture a "water closet" is not strictly correct. However, "water closet" is a fairly accurate nomenclature for the fixture when the tank-type is meant, since the tank is part of the fixture.

It is an obvious misnomer when a fixture is called a "flush-valve water closet," the type used in most public facilities where there is no closet for the water. We, that is all humans, seem unable to call that room or that fixture by any name that comes close to actually describing that function, except in the most vulgar terms that are not accepted in any but the basest societies.

Other fixtures common to that room have highly descriptive and acceptable names: "lavatory," "sink," "bathtub," "shower," and even "urinal" get said without a hint of embarrassment. But we seem to be obliged to call that fixture by the name of a more innocuous article that it emulates: "seat," "throne," "stool," "commode," and so on. Perhaps we can legitimize an old four-letter English word, "crap," and apply its derivatives to that function and room.

The Oxford English Dictionary cites the word to c. 1440 with the sense of rejected or left matter, residue, or dregs. It predates Thomas Crapper by several centuries. In any case, we in the plumbing profession, indeed the whole English-speaking world, need to select unequivocal and acceptable words for that room and that fixture. It's time to stop piddling around and get off the pot!

Chapter 2

THOMAS CRAPPER

Nestled in a bucolic setting, about 70 miles north of London, near the town of Stratford-on-Avon, surrounded by lush green fields is a small factory that makes toilet fixtures.

Many people believe that Thomas Crapper invented the flush toilet and because of that his name engendered the vulgar term for excrement. That is not true.

The OED (*Oxford English Dictionary*, the foremost authority on the English language) defines "crap" as rejected or left matter and has its first recorded use in c. 1440, long before the time of Thomas. Of course, the word was used in spoken English for many years before it appeared in writing.

The *Merriam-Webster's Collegiate Dictionary* defines the verb "crap," with less reticence than the OED, as "defecate" from 1846. Thomas Crapper lived during the Victorian era, the end of the nineteenth century. As he was supposedly born in 1837, his name could have in no way engendered the vulgar term.

No dictionary of the English language or of slang that I checked connects the word "crap" with Thomas Crapper. In private correspondence with the editors of *Merriam-Webster's Collegiate Dictionary*, I was assured that, to their knowledge, Thomas Crapper is not the origin of the word "crap."

To quote Mr. James Rader, Etymology Editor of Merriam-Webster Inc., "[T]he Victorians would hardly have tolerated a Thomas Crapper marketing toilets if his surname would have been instantly associated with a coarse word."

The British use of the word "crap" more approximates the definition given by the English *OED*, whereas it is the Americans who apply a vulgar meaning to the word as defined by the American *Merriam-Webster Dictionary*.

As for the very existence of Thomas Crapper, of the dozen or so dictionaries, encyclopedias, and source books that I have researched, only three, other than the source of the myth, mention him. The source of the myth appears to be *Flushed with Pride: The Story of Thomas Crapper* by Wallace Reyburn published in 1960.

Tom Burnam in *The Dictionary of Misinformation* (1975) connects the origin of the words "crap" and "crapper" to Thomas Crapper using the book by Wallace Reyburn as his authority. All other references to Thomas Crapper in magazine articles, papers, and studies eventually can be traced back to that same source.

As an example, an article in *Plumbing & Mechanical* (July 1986) avers that Crapper did exist. For evidence, the author cites an article in *Newsweek* of December 1, 1969. That article, however, is a review of Reyburn's book and all the "facts" stated in that article are rephrasings of Reyburn's words.

What Burnam, and most Americans, failed to recognize was that Reyburn was a British humorist and storyteller who wrote the book as an elaborate comic hoax.

The second book that mentions Thomas Crapper is Charles Panati's *Extraordinary Origins of Everyday Things*. In his book Panati traces the history of the flush toilet from 1595 without any mention of Thomas. However, in his references Panati does discuss Thomas Crapper.

He calls Reyburn's book about Crapper a hoax. He cites

another book by Reyburn about the origin of the brassiere as another hoax book. The supposed inventor of the brassiere was Otto Titzling who was biographied by Reyburn in *Bust Up: the Uplifting Tale of Otto Titzling*. A more recent book, *Thunder, Flush and Thomas Crapper* by Adam Hart-Davis, devotes several pages to Crapper, coming to the conclusion that Crapper did exist, but did not invent the flush toilet. Although Hart-Davis cites several artifacts bearing Crapper's name, all his biographical information comes from Reyburn.

Panati and H. L. Menken (*The American Language*) ascribe the invention of the modern flush toilet to John Harington, one of Elizabeth I's courtiers in 1596, but I have seen flushing toilets, which originally had wooden seats, in the ruins of the Minoan civilization in Knossos, Crete of 4000 years ago and in the ruins of Ephesus in modern Turkey dating to the early part of the first millennium.

In medieval England many abbeys had piped water for flushing toilets. Many other examples of pre-Thomas flush toilets from every century do exist. The change that came about in flush toilets during the Victorian era was that prior to John Harington's invention, flush toilets used continually flowing water to flush the waste away, or a bucket of water had to be thrown in the toilet for that purpose.

His invention was a method of storing water and

discharging a fixed amount for flushing and then having that container refilled automatically. Harington's invention was not immediately accepted.

It was during the Victorian era that other innovators devised more satisfactory methods of storing and discharging the flushing water. A most interesting source book is *Clean and Decent* by Lawrence Wright. In his book, Wright discusses the evolution of the modern toilet from its most ancient sources. Although Wright spends much time on Victorian plumbing, he does not mention Crapper at all. However, it would appear that Wright's book is the source of much of Reyburn's fiction.

Clean and Decent was published in 1960. *Flushed with Pride* was published in 1969. Many of the illustrations used in Reyburn's book appeared earlier in Wright's book. Some of the incidents cited in Reyburn's book and ascribed to Crapper are cited in Wright's book, but ascribed to others.

For example, Wright notes a test of a "sanitary closet" at the Health Exhibition of 1888. According to Wright, a Jennings "Pedistal Vase" won the gold medal by clearing "10 apples averaging 1-1/4 ins. diameter, 1 flat sponge about 4-1/2 ins. diameter, Plumber's 'smudge' coated over the pan, and 4 pieces of paper adhering closely to the soiled surface" all with a 2-gallon flush, and then testing the device by throwing in the cap of an attendant and flushing it away. Reyburn describes the same exhibition test and subsequent cap flushing in exactly the same words but intimates that it was Crapper's device that was being tested.

The editors of *Mechanical Engineering*, the magazine of the American Society of Mechanical Engineers, after a series of letters to the editor on the subject of Thomas Crapper in 1988, concluded that he never existed.

However, there is the company in England that claims to have the original chartering papers for Thomas Crapper Company, Ltd. A new owner bought the company and is making plumbing fixtures that are made according to the patterns developed by the original Crapper company.

Original Crapper factory

The new owner states that Reyburn's book about Titzling is a hoax whereas Reyburn's book about Crapper is not. Reyburn's biographical information about Thomas Crapper may have been embellished and exaggerated, but the essential facts are true.

The new owner's legal documents attesting to the original

Thomas Crapper Co., his copies of Thomas Crapper's patents and designs, all prove that Thomas Crapper did exist and made toilet fixtures.

In the basement of the Science Museum in London there is a small exhibit of household plumbing artifacts with Crapper's name on them, including a cast iron water tank clearly embossed "CRAPPER'S VALVELESS WASTE PREVENTER," but not a toilet.

The story of Crapper's invention of the flush toilet is delightful. He may have made and sold them but apparently he did not invent them. As an engineer I must flush out the facts.

Chapter 3

TOILET SEATS, UP OR DOWN?

Not all plumbing problems are amenable to engineering solutions. Some plumbing problems are not even plumbing problems. Yet, as a plumbing engineer I still get asked about them.

Take the problem of the positioning of toilet seats that has lately been a feature of advice and etiquette columns. Those columns are carrying more letters requesting an answer to the question, should toilet seats be left up or should they be put down after use? The answer has always been, put them down.

The genesis of the debate is American customary usage. When men urinate they stand and use the toilet with the seat in the up position. When men or women defecate and when women urinate, they sit and the toilet seat is in the down position. The very question asked of the advice columnists indicates that the question is directed to men. No one has ever suggested that the woman raise the toilet seat after her use.

One item of interest that is omitted from all discussions about lowering or not lowering the seat is what to do about the cover. Toilet seats and covers are sold in matching sets.   The cover is designed to cover the opening of the seat and give the toilet a finished appearance.

Women who object to men not lowering the seat after urinating should ask themselves if they ritualistically lower the cover after they use the toilet. So, as a matter of interest, I decided to look at the question of lowering or not lowering the toilet seat from an engineering (maximizing efficiency) point of view.

The first step was to establish a basis for a numerical analysis of the subject. The basis and reference for this analysis is residential use. Public toilets have different modes of operation.

The seats on women's toilets will always be in the down position. American women urinate and defecate while sitting.

Most men's public toilets have urinals as well as commodes and most men will use the urinal to urinate rather than the commode, thus the seat on the commode will almost always be in the down position.

I assume for the purpose of this analysis that both men and women defecate once and urinate five times daily. Unless there is a difference between men and women of the frequency or ratio of urination and defecation, which I have not determined, the exact frequency of toilet use is not germane to my analysis, as will become apparent.

Starting with a household of two people, one male and one female, equal frequency of use of the toilet, and alternate use thereof, an analysis of the motions of the toilet seat can be made.

Beginning in the morning with the seat up (in a moment you will see the reason for this assumption) and the proposition that the male leaves the seat up after he urinates [we can call this the A-ACAP (anti-advice columnists' accepted procedure)], the following is the sequence of operations during one day.

Female puts the seat down - defecates

Male leaves seat down - defecates

Female leaves seat down - urinates

Male raises seat - urinates

Female lowers seat - urinates

Male raises seat - urinates

Female lowers seat - urinates

Male raises seat – urinates

Female lowers seat - urinates

Male raises seat - urinates

Female lowers seat - urinates

Male raises seat - urinates, end of day.

The seat is up. You will now see the reason for my assumption that the day begins with the seat in the up position. Under this procedure the toilet seat is moved ten times during the day.

Under the same conditions and ACAP (advice columnists' accepted procedure) form of operation, whereby the male lowers the seat after his use of the toilet, the following is the sequence.

Seat is down - female defecates

Male defecates - Seat remains down

Female urinates - Seat remains down

Male raises seat - urinates - lowers seat

Female urinates - Seat remains down

Male raises seat - urinates - lowers seat

Female urinates - Seat remains down

Male raises seat - urinates - lowers seat

Female urinates - Seat remains down

Male raises seat - urinates - lowers seat

Female urinates - Seat remains down

Male raises seat - urinates - lowers seat, end of day. The seat is down.

As you can see from this analysis the seat is moved the same number times when the male moves the seat to the down position as when he does not - ten times, therefore the efficiency is the same. However, the difference is that under ACAP it is only the male who moves the toilet seat. Under A-ACAP rules the male and the female move the toilet seat an equal number of times. Of course, use of the toilet is more random than these analyses assume. However, the number of movements will not change under ACAP rules as the toilet seat always will be in the down position after each use. Therefore, there will still be ten movements of the seat: one up and one down for each male urination.

Expressed as an efficiency, no movement of the toilet seat is taken as 100% efficient (the daily total number of uses of the toilet minus the daily total number of moves of the toilet seat divided by the daily total number of uses of the toilet).

The ACAP arrangement achieves (12-10)/12 or 17% efficiency. Under the conditions of use not approved by the advice columnists (A-ACAP), random usage must be analyzed statistically.

Of the two possible positions of the toilet seat, up or down, five times out of the daily twelve uses, the seat will be left in the up position (after each male urination) and down seven times (after each female usage and male defecation). The requirement that the seat be up for the next user is also five times out of twelve (once for each male urination) and down seven times out of twelve (once for each defecation and female urination.

Thus the odds that the seat will be in the wrong position, requiring a movement of the seat for the next user is five twelfths (the odds that the next use will be a male urination) times seven twelfths (the odds that the previous user left the seat in the down position) plus seven twelfths (the odds that the next user will be a female user or a male defecator) times five twelfths (the odds that the previous user left the seat in the up position). [(5/12 X 7/12) + (7/12 X 5/12)] = 0.486.

Multiplying the odds of the seat being in the wrong position for the next user by the number of uses each day (12) is 0.486 X 12 = 5.83. Thus, if the seat is left in the last position of use, the odds are that the seat will need to be moved is only about six times a day.

We can assign an efficiency of (12-5.83)/12 or 51% to this A-ACAP arrangement. This analysis may be extended to any household with equal numbers of female and male members without affecting the results. When the ratio of females and males is changed, however, the results are changed.

Changing the number of females to two and leaving all the other factors the same, we have these daily quantities:

Female defecations - two

Male defecations - one

Female urinations - ten

Male urinations – five, for a total of eighteen uses a day.

Assuming a random use of the toilet and assuming that the male does not lower the toilet seat after each use (A-ACAP), of the two possible positions of the toilet seat, up or down, five times out of eighteen the seat will be left in the up position and down thirteen times.

The requirement that the seat be up for the next user is also five times out of eighteen, and down thirteen times out of eighteen. Thus the odds that the seat will be left in the wrong position for the next user is five eighteenths (the odds that the next use will be a male urination) times thirteen eighteenths (the odds that the previous user left the seat in the down position) plus thirteen eighteenths (the odds that the next user will be a female urinator or a defecator) times five eighteenths (the odds that the previous user left the seat in the up position. $[(5/18 \times 13/18) + (13/18 \times 5/18)] = 0.402$.

Multiplying the odds of the seat being in the wrong

position by the number of uses each day, 0.402 X 18 = 7.24. Thus, if the seat is left in the last position of use, the odds are that the seat will need to be moved is only about seven times a day or an efficiency of (18-7.24)/18 or 60%.

Under usage whereby the toilet seat is always left in the down position (ACAP), the seat will be moved ten times daily, before and after each male urination or an efficiency of 44%.

We approach equal movements of the toilet seat under each of the two procedures, ACAP or A-ACAP, or an efficiency of 100% only as we approach infinity in the ratio of females to males. If we assume a household of more males than females, the disparity between the number of times the seat is moved when the seat is left in the down position (ACAP rules) and when the seat is left in the last position of use (A-ACAP rules) is even greater because the seat will be raised and lowered for each male urination regardless of who used the toilet last or who will use it next.

Thus, we can see that the advice columnists' correct positioning of toilet seats is incorrect for reduction of effort.

But who am I, an engineer, to argue with "Dear Abby," Ann Landers, and Miss Manners when I have a wife at home and a daughter who is proofreading this article.

There are devices on the market that will help you follow the advice columnists' rules. According to a Reuters report, on sale in Germany is a devise that says "put the seat back down right away" whenever the seat is lifted.

On sale in the U. S. is a fixture to be attached to a toilet seat that lights green if the seat is down and red if the seat is up. But you needn't have traffic lights or oral warnings.   There is a device that will lower the toilet seat after it has been raised and left in the up position for an adjustable period of time. It takes 15 seconds for the seat to be lowered so you had better be finished in the allotted time or there is going to be a mess.

If you don't like the automatic operation, there is the manual (really foot) operated device that will raise and lower the toilet seat by pressing pedals with your foot.

Prisons don't have this dilemma. Prisons, both for males and females, are designed for maximum resistance to vandalism. The toilets are often made of stainless steel without toilet seats to be raised or lowered. The rim of the toilet is shaped to approximate a seat.

In the 19th century there were several designs for toilets with self-rising seats. These were probably designed by men as they put the female user at a disadvantage.

In Hong Kong an enterprising jeweler has installed gold toilets in his shop. The men's and women's toilets are made of solid gold according to the reports - the wall tiles, floors, ceilings, and, of course, the fixtures including the commodes.

The commodes are the standard European wash down type. Each toilet has a seat and a cover in the raised position as shown in photographs. I don't believe all the hype. If the seats and covers were made of solid gold as noted, once lowered, no average male or female could possibly lift them again.

At a recent home-products show, Toto USA displayed a $5,000 toilet. The toilet flushes automatically, the seat is heated, and it is self-cleaning. No word on whether the seat is lowered automatically.

According other news reports, a proposal has been made, not so much as to solve the toilet seat positioning problem, but if accepted, will do just that. Young women in Sweden, Germany, and Australia have a new cause: they want men to sit down while urinating. This demand comes partly from concerns about hygiene—avoiding the splash factor—but, more crucially, because a man standing up to urinate is deemed to be triumphing in his masculinity, and by extension, degrading women.

One argument that has been expressed for having men sit to urinate is that if women can't do it, then men shouldn't either. Another is that standing upright while relieving oneself is a "nasty macho gesture," suggestive of male violence.

An equally vociferous group of women in the U. S. are promoting the concept of women learning to urinate while standing, even using men's urinals. There is a fascinating website that describes the technique, including details on how to do it without undressing by unzipping the fly on one's jeans. Does this foretell a future where men sit and women stand?

Chapter 4

WOMEN'S URINALS

While the campaign to have men lower the toilet seat after each use is continuing, there is another counter-campaign in operation, that is, to teach women to urinate standing up.

The campaign to get women in the U. S. and Western Europe to urinate standing up is not new. In the Muslim culture, women are expected to stand to urinate. This stricture dates to Mohammed's time and is included with the requirement for men to squat while urinating.

This actually is a pre-Muslim custom in the Middle-East that was reported by Herodotus who wrote in the fifth century B. C., "The women stand up when they make water." Later, in Richard Burton's translation of *A Thousand Nights and a Night* (1865) he says, "In the East women stand on minor occasions," confirming that it was a Muslim custom at that time.

It also was common during the Middle Ages in Europe if we are to take Ken Follet's description of a scene in his *The Pillars of the Earth* as being accurate. He wrote, "'Piss on the Rule of St. Benedict!' she yelled at the top of her voice. Then she hitched up her skirt, bent her knees and urinated on the open book." From this we can determine two things. Women commonly urinated in a standing position and that women commonly wore no under garments.

Perhaps this can explain why in the 19th century a toilet seat was devised that automatically raised itself after use.

This is just the opposite of the self-lowering toilet seats being touted today. If, at that time, women commonly urinated standing up, and there is at least one website that advocates such action and proposes to teach women how to use a men's urinal, such a toilet seat would make sense.

A while ago, our local newspaper ran an article on the recent invention of a woman's urinal. When they found some interest in the subject, they came to me for an opinion. They interviewed me and reported on my comments as a Professional Engineer. The result was published with my photograph (*Florida Today*: November 8, 1993).

I felt then, and do now, that in Western society such a device would not be generally acceptable. Women in Western society are trained to sit when they urinate. To stand while they do that is felt to be unnatural. In some other societies it is different, the most notable being the Muslim culture. This chapter will be limited to Western society.

There are good engineering and economic reasons to incorporate women's urinals in the design of public facilities. Urinals would appear to be more sanitary than the traditional water closet. The woman would not touch the fixture just as a man does not touch the urinal. Restrooms may be kept cleaner as the fixture is smaller than a water closet and thus easier to clean around.

Maintenance costs would be less. As there is no seat, there is no seat to be damaged or destroyed. The water flow rate for a typical modern water closet is 30 gpm (gallons per minute) and 20 gpm for a urinal. The latest requirements for total flow for each flush are 1.6 gallons for a toilet and one gallon for a urinal. Without going into a detailed mathematical calculation, it is obvious that by converting women to urinal usage, a great deal of savings can be made in piping sizes and water usage and sewage requirements.

This is something that both environmentalists and water departments should champion. It is presumed that the urinal, being easier and faster to use, would have a quicker user turnaround time thus requiring fewer units, or enabling shorter lines between acts at the opera.

Regardless of all the good reasons for installing women's urinals, I do not believe in their general acceptance in the western world and that is primarily because of the "unnatural" position that the woman would be required to assume in using the fixture.

There is historical precedent for my opinion. In the not-too-distant past, various plumbing fixture manufacturers tried to introduce women's urinals. Although they were manufactured and listed in catalogs for several years, not many were installed. In the course of my business, I have been in many public women's toilets, probably more than most women, yet I have never seen one with a urinal.

In the forties and fifties of the last century several manufacturers of toilet fixtures, especially two of the most prominent, American Standard and Kholer, came out with women's urinals.

American Standard made the "Sanistand" from 1950 to 1973. Kohler made the "Hygia." They were not a great success and were discontinued soon after. There are leftovers of those fixtures still to be found installed around the U. S. In the 1952 American Standard plumbing fixture catalog, six pages are devoted to the "Sanistand" women's urinals.

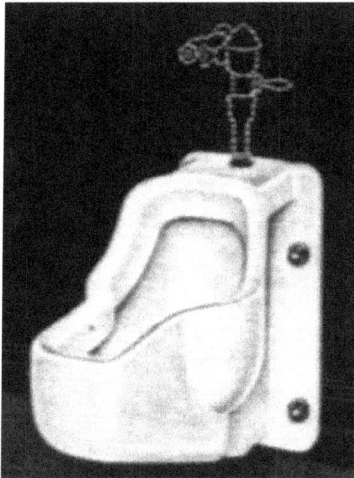

Sanistand

The urinals are similar to the type of men's urinal that is wall hung and has a lip that comes out of the center bottom. The women's urinal has a similar lip but it protrudes further, allowing the woman to straddle it in use.

Kohler of Kohler made similar fixtures called "Hygia" which are shown in their 1956 catalog.

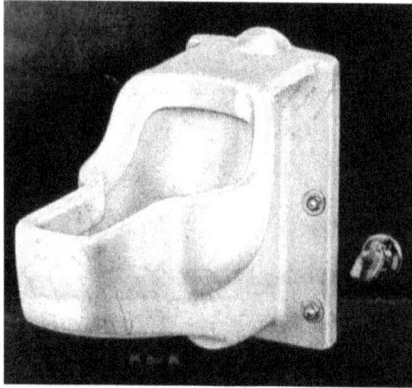

Hygia

Other manufacturers also made women's urinals. I have seen fixtures in men's toilets that look just like the illustrations in the catalogs. I suspect that those fixtures were purchased and installed as women's urinals, but when they failed in their intended use they were switched to the men's toilets.

The description of the use of the fixture in the American Standard catalog may point to two reasons for the failure of acceptance of the fixture. Decals were provided with the fixture for posting in the toilet to describe how to use the fixture. The Sanistand urinal is installed in a private enclosure, just like a water closet. The user backs up to the fixture and straddles it. But she need not sit down or touch the fixture in any way.

The Sanistand serves the purpose of a water closet and

urinal and offers the highest degree of sanitation demanded by women customers and employees. The position described is untenable. The woman should face the wall just as men do. When a woman urinates, the stream is forward and down. A woman who is somewhat queasy about using an unfamiliar fixture may not back up far enough and thus overshoot the lip and create a mess on the floor. As the back (wall-side) of the fixture is higher and wider than the lip, the possibility of missing the mark is much less than when facing the fixture.

The second difficulty occurs in its intended use. The catalog says, "Large outlet. Permits napkin and tissue disposal and allows the fixture to serve the same purpose as a water closet, if necessary." The designer of the urinal and the writer of the catalog recognized that the urinal may be used as a water closet. Men's urinals have no provision for passing any solid matter; even cigarette butts do not go down the drain. A urinal should be designed to be a urinal, not a combination urinal and toilet.

From an early age, once they leave the potty, males stand when urinating. They learn to separate the urinating and defecating functions. A man can control his bowels when urinating. It is not that women cannot do this, they can and do, but they are not trained to do it. Women, in a sense, never leave the potty. Faced with the need to urinate, will she deliberately control the last sphincter muscle on her digestive system? I think not, and the manufacturer of the Sanistand apparently also did not.

It is certainly possible to train women to use a urinal. Such training would have to begin at an early age and must be given by mothers who themselves are trained in the use of urinals. Is it worth the effort and expense required to institute such training? What would be gained by it? I, for one, do not think that a woman's urinal would be useful in Western society.

Since that interview and newspaper article several years ago, I have not seen any reference to that particular woman's urinal. It has quietly passed away as have other recent attempts at selling a woman's urinal. Recently, a new wave of women's urinals has been promoted by several manufacturers.

A Dutch company has introduced a product called a "Lady P." The urinals from the fifties and most of those of recent manufacture are comparable in shape and use. They are similar to a man's urinal with a narrow, extended lip that a woman is supposed to straddle.

In their advertisements for the Lady P, a woman is shown using the urinal with her back to the wall. In this case the protrusion from the wall appears to be less than the women's urinals of fifty years ago, thus making it more difficult to use it while facing the wall.

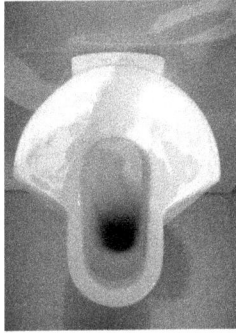

The Lady P

No mention is made of using the urinal for defecation or disposal of sanitary napkins. Although this type of woman's urinal may have worked well a hundred years ago when it was not too widespread for women to wear underwear (panties), it becomes less tenable now with women commonly wearing pants both as an undergarment and as an outer garment. I predict that this type of women's urinal, too, will fail.

To get around that clothing problem, a different approach in urinal design for women has been attempted by some manufacturers. The "She-inal" is typical of several manufacturers' products that use a funnel-like device attached to a hose to collect the urine.

When this product first came out in 1993, I was interviewed by *Florida Today* for my opinion of it. I said then that I felt that it would not be acceptable for most women.

Using the She-inal

1. Use handle to lift and rotate cone.

2. Place a sanitary paper guard over top rim of cone.

3. Adjust clothing out of way and step up to cone. Stand directly above cone.

4. Rehang cone and flush. Guard will drop as you hang cone in holder.

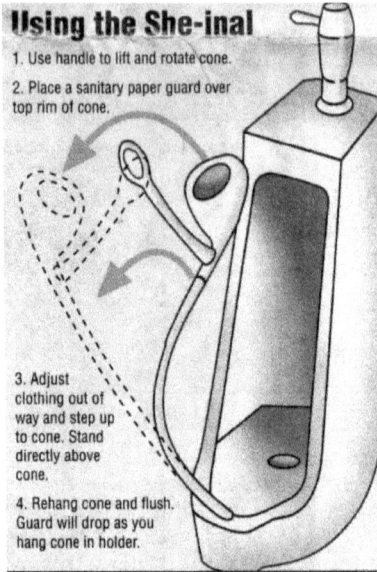

The She-inal is no longer being manufactured. I don't believe that the current crop of similar women's urinals will survive either. The main objection to the She-inal and similar devices is how they are supposed to be used. If a woman is squeamish about using a public toilet seat and thus requires paper seat covers, or one of the more elaborate seat cleaning or covering devices described before, how will she feel about using a cup-like device pressed against her body?

There is one successful but very limited funnel and hose-type urinal in use. Used by both men and women it is aboard the Space Shuttle, the Space Station, and MIR.

Chapter 5

WHERE DO YOU GO WHEN YOU GOTTA GO?

In the chapter "Toilet Seats, Up or Down" I proposed an engineering solution to the on-going question that was the title of the article. Although I did mention that the genesis of the problem is the American customary usage of men standing when they urinate, I did not emphasize that the problem is almost completely confined to the Americas and Europe, which for this purpose includes Australia and New Zealand.

To restate Julius Caesar, the world is divided into three types of toilets. There are the Western styles, on which we sit when we defecate; the Eastern styles, over which one squats while defecating; and all the rest.

Western

The Western style was fully established in ancient times. In the palace of Sargon the Great of Babylon (c. 2500 B. C.) there were six sitting toilets that discharged into a sewer about one meter high.

In excavations of the Minoan civilization of 2000 B. C. on Crete, indoor toilet facilities have been uncovered. These facilities consist of holes in stone slabs mounted at sitting height with wooden seats, similar to those currently found in outhouses in many parts of this country.

Running water flowed in troughs beneath the slabs to wash away the waste. Similar facilities have been uncovered at Ephesus and elsewhere in ruins dating from the Roman era. The oldest known flushable indoor toilets were found at Skara Brae on Mainland, the largest of the Orkney Islands in Scotland.

Those toilets date from about 6000 years ago. Not much is known about the toilets, whether they were of the Western or Eastern style, where the water came from for flushing, but they do have sewer drains indicating that they were flushed.

A flush toilet has been reported to have been found in a tomb in China. This 2000-year-old toilet appears to be Western style with a stone seat, running water, and an armrest. It is dated from the time of the Western Han Dynasty (206 B.C. to 24 A.D.). It would seem that the ancient Chinese believed that the spirits of the dead performed the normal bodily functions.

Four thousand years ago in the Indus Valley of modern

Pakistan, flushing toilets were used. One thousand years ago many abbeys in Britain had flushing toilets. A monastery in Canterbury, England had indoor plumbing in 1165. It was in Thomas Jefferson's administration that flush toilets were added to the White House.

The first public toilet appeared in London in 1852. The cost for using it was one penny from which the British expression "to spend a penny" meaning to go to the toilet was derived.

The Globe Theater of Shakespeare had no toilet facilities. Patrons seated in the balconies, which were attached to the circular walls of the theater, would wander over to the nearby Thames River to relieve themselves. Patrons standing in the pit (the open area in front of the stage where there were no seats), who were almost entirely men, would often urinate where they were standing while watching the show, rather than lose their place.

Modern versions of western toilets, consisting of open seats over pools of water, which are flushed out after each use, come in many variations. The major difference among them is the size and shape of the water pool. The larger the water surface, sometimes called the water spot, the less likelihood there is of staining of the sides of the vessel with excreta.

The main purpose of the water pool is to cover the feces which would generate odors if exposed to air. In this respect American toilets are generally superior to those made in other countries. Most American toilets work on the symphonic principle. That is, water is emptied into the bowl until the level of the water is above the siphon outlet in the back.   When the water reaches that height, the siphon fills and the water in the bowl empties in a rush. In some cases, the water enters the bowl from the front below the water surface and helps push the contents of the bowl out.

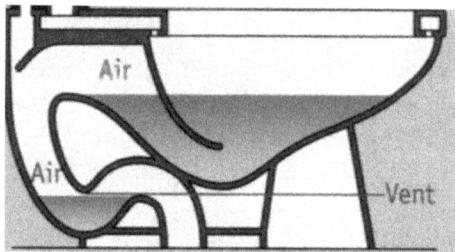

The other common toilet in use in the United States is the blowout type. The blowout type of toilet uses the pressure of the water supply to push the contents of the bowl out of the fixture. The blowout type is much noisier than the symphonic type and thus is not commonly used in residences.   Also, in order to utilize the line water pressure to move the contents of the bowl, it is directly connected to the water line through a flush valve rather than through a tank.

Instead of having a relatively deep and wide pool of water in which to deposit the excrement, in France and most other European countries, the most common toilet is a funnel shaped device with only a small pool of water at the bottom providing only a small target area. The small amount of water in the pool does not allow for symphonic action of the trap.   The incoming water pushes out the contents of the bowl.   Staining of the sides is common. Operation is similar to the American blowout toilet.

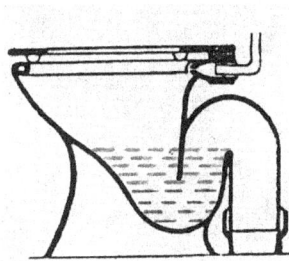

Instead of having a relatively deep pool of water in which to deposit the excrement, the most common German toilet has a shelf on which there is about a half an inch of water. On this shelf the feculence is placed. Although this arrangement allows odors to escape, it does allow for easy examination of the stool, which may be its primary purpose. This pattern is found in most homes.

Public and hotel toilets generally follow the French pattern. The symphonic action of the typical American toilet requires a smaller trap than the washdown or washout action of the European designs; thus clogging of the toilet is more common in the U. S. than in Europe, and staining more common in Europe.

The difference between the American designs and the European designs is sometimes expressed as the difference between a brush and a plunger. It is not uncommon for a plunger to be found in the American home toilet room whereas European toilet rooms usually have toilet brushes available.

Now most industrialized countries have codes that mandate a maximum of 1.6 gallons of water for each flush of the toilet. In the U. S., the old limit was five gallons until 1980 when a limit of 4 gallons was imposed. That limit was lowered to 3.5 gallons until 1994 when the 1.6-gallon limit went into effect.

We will see changes in the design of both American and

European toilets as the technology and restrictions expand.

Eastern

Squatting while defecating is probably the oldest position a human uses. Dogs, cats, monkeys, and apes do it. There is no reason to think that our ancestors did not. So it is not inconceivable that when fixtures were first made for that purpose, that they were made for squatting over rather than sitting on.

In most of Asia and the Middle East, toilet facilities consist of fixtures at floor level. There are two major versions of these fixtures. In the Middle East and Japan, the toilets are essentially holes in the ground. In the non-Chinese version, the holes are usually round, about four inches in diameter, but may be oblong and larger.

The holes are usually cast in concrete or are in porcelain slabs of about two-foot square size. The slabs are sloped to the hole with raised foot-pedals in front of the hole. Often there are no flushing capabilities although flush tanks and flush valves are common.

The typical Chinese toilet is a porcelain fixture about six inches wide and eighteen inches long, buried to its rim in a raised platform about four to six inches high and placed perpendicular to a wall. The interior of the fixture is a concave half-cylinder. The fixture is dry except when flushed.

At the outer end, the porcelain is formed into a raised catch basin similar to the training potties that we use for our children. The fixtures are connected to flush valves or overhead tanks. Many of the porcelain fixtures have flushing rims.

There are no seats with the Eastern style toilets; the fixture is used by squatting over it. As there are no seats to adjust, vandalize, or become filthy, and no part of the bare body touches any part of the facility, use of the Oriental toilet may be considered more sanitary than use of the Western toilet.

In some public toilets the fixtures are arrayed in banks with no partitions between them. Other public toilets do have partitions and some even have doors on the partitions. Men's and women's toilets are the same. Men's public toilets may also have stand-up urinals.

In China, both Western-style toilets and Chinese-style toilets are found. New hotels in China, which are designed for foreign tourists and business travelers, have standard American-style toilets in their guestrooms. In fact, most of the toilets seem to be made by American Standard. Some hotels even have the latest low-flow types.

But out on "the economy" the story is different. With few exceptions, public toilets are Chinese-style. Where foreigners are expected, such as in some department stores, special stores catering to foreigners, and some tourist sites like the Jade Temple in Shanghai, some toilets may be American-style.

Soft-seat (first class) railroad cars have an American-style toilet at one end and a Chinese-style toilet at the other. In the railroad cars, the toilets are formed of stainless steel. The effluent of the toilets drops directly on to the railroad tracks.

In a typical farmhouse in China that I visited, the toilet consisted of two rectangular slabs of rock spaced about four inches apart over a depression in the ground. The shape is a precursor of the Chinese-style toilets. The deposits are shoveled out and used for fertilizer.

In China, public or group toilets often consist of a trench about eight inches wide and eight inches deep made of concrete and, in the more upscale places, tile-lined, and of any length, running parallel to one wall.

Some public toilets have partitions that divide the trench into sections, but the effluent still flows from section to section. For example, in one railway station that I visited, the toilet consisted of a row of enclosed stalls with doors. There was a trench in the concrete floor in which water continuously flowed. The trench ran from stall to stall. The user squatted over the trench, not facing the door but sideways, where he or she could observe what had been deposited in the trench upstream. The slit trench, without the water, should be familiar to anyone who served in the army.

In one pre-school that I visited, the one toilet room for the children contained a long trench on one side the full length of the room, about 15 feet, with a hand rail on the wall for balance, and a trough urinal on the opposite wall.

Chinese pre-school bathroom, boys' side

At a break in their lessons, about two dozen girls and boys raced into the toilet. The girls squatted over the trench on one side of the room and the boys stood at the urinal on the other side.

Chinese pre-school bathroom, girls' side

All the girls faced the same direction over the trench. I was told that toilets for the sexes are not separated until the children enter regular school at about six years of age.

For a Westerner to use an Eastern-style toilet often incurs some difficulty. The squatting position is difficult to obtain unless the person is particularly limber or has been doing it since his youth.

The tendons in the back of the leg must stretch to achieve the proper position with the heels on the ground and the rear end directly over the small hole or trench. I have known Americans who have reported falling over trying to use a Japanese toilet.

Orientals also have difficulty in using western toilets. Many an Oriental will squat, with his or her feet on the rim of the bowl, to use a Western toilet. That sort of begs the question of whether the seat should be lowered after use. At a department store in Shinjuku, Tokyo, which had both Western and Eastern toilets, there were instructions in each stall with a Western toilet on how to use it.

Even so, some medical authorities have suggested that the Eastern-style toilet is better than the Western. It would seem that difficult evacuation is eased when the squatting position is used. Eastern-style toilets are found occasionally in France. Some of the older brasseries and newer train stations have them as an option.

The public toilets that replaced the older *pisoires* have an Eastern-style toilet with a bar that can be lowered to sit upon. They are easier to clean and resist vandalism better than a Western-style toilet.

Other or None

Most of the Western and Eastern toilets described above use water to flush the excrement. But there are many exceptions.

The standard American outhouse uses no water. It is a sitting-type toilet over a dry pit. Some European castles had sitting-type toilets that protruded outside the castle walls. The excrement dropped directly into the castle's moat. No doubt the purpose was to make attacking the castle more unpleasant.

Some squatting toilets in the Middle East are like American outhouses. They are dry over a pit.

There are other possibilities. In the non-urban Middle East an entirely different approach is used. Nomadic peoples, such as the Bedouin Arabs, have no need for permanent toilet facilities and therefore no need for toilet fixtures. An open area outside the temporary camp or along the route of march is sufficient. A small hole is dug and the deposit immediately covered with sand.

In small villages a communal toilet is provided which consists of a depression in the ground surrounded by reed screening. When filled, the hole is covered with sand, the reed screening is moved to a different location and a new hole is dug.

In cities and towns that have waste disposal systems, the Eastern hole-in-the-floor fixture is used. When it comes to the Middle East, primarily the Arabian Peninsula and the Bedouins, we come as far from European and Oriental practices as it is possible to be.

I quote from a note in Richard Burton's translation of *A Thousand Nights and a Night* (1865). In the East women stand on minor occasions while the men squat on their hunkers in a way hardly possible to an untrained European. Burton further quotes Herodotus about Arabia, who wrote in the fifth century B. C., "The women stand up when they make water, but the men sit down. To ensure proper modesty, men and women remain fully covered by their clothing when urinating or defecating." I can vouch that the second part of Herodotus' statement is still valid.

This practice was strongly brought to my attention when I was in charge of designing the Saudi-Arabian Air Force Academy at Al-Kharj. There are no urinals in this all-male institution. We were directed by the Saudi liaison not to put any in the academy.

As for the first part of the statement, I am assured by a woman with personal knowledge that that practice is also still valid. The practice of women standing to urinate was probably also a European custom in the Dark Ages. In Ken Follett's book *The Pillars of the Earth* he describes a scene where "Ellen hitched up her skirt, bent her knees, and urinated on the open book."

Two facts can be deduced from this quotation. One, women commonly urinated in a standing position if Ellen was able to do it so readily. Two, women in the twelfth century, as in contemporary Arab dress, wore no undergarments.

On the San Blas islands of Panama, toilet practice is also far from the Western mode. The Cuna Indians do not defecate or urinate on land. When needed, they wade or swim out into the ocean, which surrounds them, and then perform their egestions.

For tourists, who are not prepared to join the natives in deep or shallow water, outhouse-type facilities are provided. However, on looking down through the hole in seat, one sees not a lime-filled pit, but the open ocean.

The Choco Indians, who live inland of the Cuna Indians, also do not urinate or defecate on the land. They use the rivers upstream of their villages for the females and downstream for the males.

The Indians of the rain forest of Peru also have no toilets. The forest is everywhere around their homes. When they have to go, they do what every hunter and farmer does: step behind a tree or bush. No toilets or toilet seats there. That is the situation in much, if not most, of the agricultural and rural world.

In the agricultural world, a toilet similar to the Chinese one is often used. The decomposed or decomposing feces is a-periodically extracted and dispersed on the farm fields as fertilizer.

Where no such facility exists, they do what the Choco Indians do. In non-rural and urban areas, in undeveloped counties and alleys in developed countries, excretion is unceremoniously deposited in streets, alleys and open spaces.

In the past, in homes where toilets did not exist, chamber pots were used.

Chamber pot

They would be emptied every morning often by tossing their contents out the window on to the street with the warning, *"garde l'eau"* ("watch out for the water") which became the British slang for a toilet: "loo."

From these streets, the effluent eventually found its way to the nearest river.

Privacy

In the Western world, in public toilets, privacy is assumed for defecation. Western-style commodes, and Eastern-style squatters, when they are used, are enclosed in stalls with doors.

Urinals for men are generally not placed in stalls but mounted on walls open to view from anywhere in the men's room.

Wall-mounted troughs are occasionally seen in public men's rooms in the U. S. and U.K.

Troughs in the floor are more common.

In recent years, partition screens between individual urinals are appearing more and more.

In the old *pisoires* of France, someone outside the convenience could see the heads and feet of the men inside, and thus could surmise what was going on inside, but the men inside could see what the other men were doing.

Going back in history to Skara Brae, Minos, Babylon, and Ephesus, we can see banks of sitting toilets without partitions between. In the U. S. Army basic training barracks during WWII, the arrangement was similar.

In the Middle-East, urinating and defecating is a sprightly private affair. Where toilets are provided, they are constructed with stalls and doors. The partitions do not have spaces between the partitions and the floor.

In the desserts, people will move away from the camp to do what is necessary. Even so, they remain completely covered. Not wearing anything under their outer clothing, they remain unexposed.

In the Far East, Chinese public toilets were and are of the gang type, ranks of squatters without partitions or partitions without doors, for men and women.

Chapter 6

POTTY PARITY

We all have observed the long lines outside the women's toilets at the intermissions of theatrical shows, concerts, sporting events, and other congregations. Even when there is no periodic cessation of activities, there are often lines at women's toilets, but not at men's. Airports come to mind, but it is occasionally true at shopping centers, filling stations, and restaurants as well.

This was not always the case. When Western society was primarily agrarian, that problem did not exist. Rarely were there large congregations of women, with or without men.   In fact, public toilets are a manifestation of modern urban society. Public toilets in an agricultural milieu were the nearest field or forest, open equally to men and women.

As society became urbanized, women were more confined to home and hearth. They did not, at first, attend public performances in great numbers. Even the parts of women were played by men in Shakespeare's time. Public toilet facilities, if provided at all, were usually provided only for men.

At the Globe Theater in Shakespeare's London no toilet facilities were provided. There were but few women in the audience. There were many in the third-tier balcony, but they were not there to watch the plays. Men, who had seats in the balconies, would leave the theater when it became necessary and walk over to the nearby Thames River to urinate or defecate. Those standing in the pit, almost entirely men, would often urinate where they were standing rather than lose their place by going to the Thames.

A notorious example of provisions for men only were the succinctly labeled *pissoires* placed on all the grand boulevards and public spaces of Paris and other cities in France. That existed until much after the end of the Second World War. These were structures whose function was aptly denoted by their name. They usually consisted of a cylindrical, cast-iron column over which water flowed into a trough at the bottom that carried away the waste to a sewer. Several men at a time could stand around the column. To hide the men using the facility from view, outside the interior column there was a black iron skirting that enclosed the annular space in which the men stood. The outer shield was spaced about two feet from the inner column and had one or two openings through which a man could enter the inner space. Sometimes the skirting sported advertising posters. The outer shield extended from below a man's knees to above a Frenchman's head.

A tall Frenchman or an American would have his head above the shield, and everyone's feet were visible. A few *pissoires* had rain covers. Few public facilities were provided for women and these were usually underground, such as the magnificent 1905 Art Nouveau facility adjacent to the Church of the Madeleine. Unfortunately, that facility is now closed.

There is at least one such facility still in use in the French city of Quebec. It is only a half-round facility attached to a wall, but it is a standard *pissoire,* never the less.

In smaller cities, towns, and villages in France and in many other continental countries, other facilities were provided. Usually they were ceramic, full-height urinals mounted on building walls. Often small projecting wings were attached to provide some degree of privacy.

In Chartres, France, a urinal without protective wings is installed on the side of the cathedral adjacent to the main square. I don't think that we should make any religious or political significance out of the act of urinating on the side of a church. Of course, no comparable facilities were provided for the women.

Yet France, with its public facilities, in previous times was considered far advanced over other countries in Europe and America for its provision of public sanitary facilities. We may decry the unequal arrangements for men and women that existed only forty or fifty years ago, but the arrangements reflected society of the time.

In France, until recently, there were many public facilities for men, because in general, women did not parade the *Grandes Boulevards* of Paris, male *boulevardiers* did. Women did not attend sporting events; men did. Women did not go to the Moulin Rouge; men did.

The few women that did go to the opera, a restaurant, a ball, or the theater generally were escorted by men, not alone. How they got to their seats in the Barcelona bullring through the open urinal, that was the tunnel under the seats, without seeing the hundreds of men standing there and urinating against the wall, I can't imagine. Perhaps they did see them but didn't "notice."

The same thing may have been true as they walked the *Champs Élysées* on the arms of their escorts. In any event, men urinated where they would. Women, only at home. The French in recent years have replaced the male-only *pissoires* with more modern facilities for both men and women, and in doing so have pointed a way to a solution of our potty parity problem.

Where each funereal black *pissoire* previously stood they placed a gleaming stainless-steel structure.

The same locations were used because the water supply and drainage were already there. There is one entrance to the small building and entry is gained by depositing a coin in a slot. It is available to men and women equally.

Only one person is expected to enter at one time. The inside is completely tile-lined. The toilet is a stainless-steel eastern-style unit with a lowerable bar for those who prefer to sit. After each use the whole interior is automatically sprayed and washed down with water.

Other older non-automatic public facilities are guarded by a *functionaire* whose sole purpose seems to be the collection of a small *pourboire*. Through this entrance both men and women pass. Once past the attendant there are a series of stalls for the use of either men or women on one side and wash basins on the other. The stalls have enclosures that go to the floor and contain a standard water closet.

Beyond the stalls or around a corner are a line of urinals. In other words, except for the urinals, a unisex toilet. The price for use of the stalls is double that for use of the urinals. More recently, some of those stainless-steel structures are being removed and are being replaced by public toilets inside buildings and underground, no doubt in order to make them less conspicuous.

In the U. S., in order to alleviate the lines at women's

toilets, we hear cries calling for increasing the number of toilets for women. The minimum number of toilets provided in any public facility is governed by code, and since equality of men and women is assumed, the number of facilities required has been equal for men and women.

For example, the Standard Plumbing Code, previously effective in Florida, mandated a minimum of 4 water closets for men and 4 water closets for women for a theater of 200 seats. Urinals are counted as water closets. Similarly, a theater of 200 seats in Britain, as cited in *Thunder, Flush and Thomas Crapper* by Adam Hart-Davis, required one water closet and four urinals for males and seven water closets for females.

Recently, various code-writing authorities have come to recognize that absolute equivalency in the number of fixtures assigned to male and female users does not satisfy the actual traffic patterns.

One reason for that is contained in a study, where it was calculated that women spend, on average, 80 seconds using a public toilet and men spend only 45 seconds. Potty parity is no longer the ultimate goal. For example, The International Plumbing Code, now in effect in Florida, generally mandates about twice as many toilets for women as toilets plus urinals for men in the larger venues.

The American Society of Plumbing Engineers (ASPE) has

proposed a project to determine just how many urinals and water closets are required for males and females in public buildings. There is plenty of anecdotal information on the relationship of the number of water closets and urinals to the number of people in attendance, but true analytical research has been done.

Nothing prevents the architect or owner of a facility to design in additional toilet facilities, except for the expense. In some existing facilities, it is unusual to find a strict code ratio. The following are some examples of the number of toilets provided for men and women in various facilities (figures for New York toilets are from *The Toilets of New York* by Ken Eichenbaum). In this listing, urinals are counted as water closets.

FACILITY	MEN	WOMEN
Brevard Art Museum	3	2
Surfside Playhouse	4	4
Bernard's Surf Sports Bar	4	2
BBC Planetarium	6	6
Central Park Zoo	6	6
N. Y. Public Library	11	10
Grand Central Station	16	20
Saks Fifth Avenue	11	19
Bloomingdale's	7	30

Justification for the imbalance of the number of facilities for a sports bar or a women's store is rational, but why the imbalance in a museum? If it were allowed, utilizing the French model and combining men's and women's toilets into a unisex toilet would go a long way toward achieving the desired elimination of the long lines for using the women's room.

That arrangement would still give the men some advantage, as they would have access to more facilities than the women would have. To offset that advantage, in a unisex toilet, the women would be in the same line as the men and would have the same wait as a man.

But, Americans are loath to use unisex toilets. Indeed, there are codes and regulations that prohibit it. In designing the underground Command Center for the Strategic Air Command at Offutt Air Base in Nebraska, we had a problem to solve. The Command Center was a small two-story building built completely underground, therefore space was at a premium.

The second floor contained banks of computers that were serviced by only one or two people. Regulations required that they be provided with toilet facilities.   Regulations also required that, since the one or two operators could be either male or female, we had to provide separate toilet facilities. It took months of going up the chain of command to get permission to provide only one toilet facility for the one or two people that might need to use it.

We Americans have no difficulty in the use of unisex toilets in our homes, but are repelled by a suggestion that they be used in public. This is in spite of their accepted use in airplanes, on busses, and at temporary outdoor functions such as carnivals. I would think that in locations of high usage where waiting lines could be expected (such as arenas, theaters, and airline terminals), the use of unisex toilets would be a cost-effective way of alleviating the waiting-line problem.

Chapter 7

GREAT HOUSES

M any of the great houses of this world have interesting tales to tell. Most of the tales are told by the tour guides and are included in the brochures and books sold in their gift shops. There are other tales and stories that are not told, and may not even be known to the guides and writers of the guidebooks.

As a plumbing engineer I sometimes note things in these great houses that pass by the uninitiated. These items do not necessarily say anything, but can give a person insight into to the character and culture of the owner and designer. I will not interpret these findings for you. I will point them out and let you make of them what you will.

Biltmore House is cited as the largest home in the United States. Located near Asheville, North Carolina, it was completed in 1889. Commissioned by George Vanderbilt, grandson of "Commodore" Cornelius Vanderbilt, it contains 250 rooms, including 32 guestrooms. "Ever mindful of his guests' comfort, Vanderbilt equipped his home with central heating, mechanical refrigeration, electric lights and appliances, and indoor bathrooms—unheard of luxuries at the time," says the descriptive brochure.

Included in the many "modern" amenities built into the mansion are many flush toilets: adjacent to each master and guest bedroom, by the indoor swimming pool, in the Bachelors' Wing, and several other places.

In the basement, near the kitchen where there is water and drain piping in place for food preparation, there are sleeping accommodations for the head cook. However, his room had no toilet, only a chamber pot and no washing facilities. This was for the man who handled all the food for the Vanderbilts and their guests. There are also no toilet facilities for the rest of the kitchen staff, although they could probably use the kitchen sinks to wash their hands.

John and Mable Ringling's home, Ca d'Zan ("John's House" in the Venetian dialect), near Sarasota, Florida is not as grand as the Biltmore mansion. At only 30 rooms, it is still a grander home than most of us would aspire to have. The building was completed in 1926.

As is typical of great houses, John and Mable had separate bedroom suites. Each had its own toilet room; his includes a barber chair and an exercise room. His bathtub, a massive affair to accommodate his bulk, consists of a solid block of yellow Sienna marble, carved out to form a tub.

Her tub is also marble, but consists of slabs assembled in the shape of a tub, a much less expensive construction.

You all know about Versailles, the great French Chateau occupied and enlarged for Louis XIV in 1682. It is the symbol of elegance, nobility, and extravagance. During the glorious reign of the Sun King, the magnificent palace of Versailles had no toilets.

The royals and nobles used chamber pots that were emptied by their servants. The servants, hangers-on, and others around and about the palace often used the halls and corridors for urinating and defecating, and it was used perhaps for emptying the nobles' chamber pots. The corridors were so filthy that the nobles could not walk through the mess of the halls and instead had to be carried in litters from room to room over the ordure.

Incidentally, the practice of using a small room adjacent to the main guest room for dressing and cleaning, as well as where the chamber pot was kept and used, is the origin of our word "toilet," *toile* being the French word for "cloth," *toilette* being the French word for one's dress, and by extension, where one dressed. Both we and the French still use the word "toilet" to mean the process of grooming and dressing.

Chapter 8

TOILET PAPER

After the publication of my article on the positioning of toilet seats, I was challenged by several readers to put my research and analytical skills to the equally vexing and contentious problem of how a toilet paper roll should be mounted in its holder.

The question is: should the paper roll be mounted so that the loose end hangs down in the front (away from the wall, or AFW) or to the back (against the wall, or AW)? This question did not arise until recently.

Probably in pre-agrarian society leaves were used. In Southern colonial America, corn cobs were frequently the product of choice. Urban societies depended on newspapers. With the coming of the mail-order catalog, the Sears & Roebuck catalog was hung in most outhouses in rural America.

Newspapers and catalogs were so readily available that the sale of toilet paper was limited by the competition of a free alternative.

At first, toilet paper came in sheets as early as 1718 and is still commonly sold that way in Europe. It wasn't until 1882 that rolls of toilet paper became available, and in the U. S., virtually eliminated the sheet form of toilet paper and engendered the question that is the subject of this chapter.

Careful observation of toilet paper in the United States has led to the determination of two variables that affect the answer to this question. The two factors in this analysis are the appearance of the paper and the design of the paper holder.

1. Appearance - Toilet paper comes in two types that are germane to this study: a) printed, b) non-printed.

2. Holders - Toilet paper holders come in four types: a) free standing, b) cantilevered from the wall, c) recessed into the wall, d) hinged at the wall.

Appearance.

Examination of toilet paper rolls found in supermarkets in the U. S. has failed to reveal any printed toilet paper that is printed on both sides or that is printed on the side other than that which is rolled on the outside. Therefore, although such types of toilet paper may exist, they are so uncommon that they may be ignored in this discussion. So, for this study, printed toilet paper means paper printed on the outside of the roll.

All samples of colored toilet paper examined showed color on both sides of the paper, therefore colored paper was not treated as a separate category in this study, but is classified with unprinted toilet paper.

Toilet papers are sometimes embossed. The embossing shows on both sides of the paper, but is meant to be read from the side on the outside of the roll, therefore embossing does not create a category different from those listed above and is considered the same as printed paper.

Holders

Free-standing - Some free-standing toilet paper holders

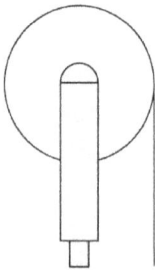

are designed in such a manner that it is difficult to access the free end of the paper unless it is loaded so that the free end hangs on the user's side, thus making the making the question of the direction of loading non-moot. The toilet paper roll is mounted directly above the vertical rod, thus the free end must hang towards the front.

Other free-standing holders are of the cantilever- or hinged-type and are considered with those types.

The other three classes of toilet paper holders do allow for a choice of the mounting position of the toilet paper.

Cantilevered from the wall - The cantilevered holder allows for the toilet paper roll to be mounted with the free end AW (Against the Wall) or AFW (Away from the Wall). If the toilet paper roll is mounted AFW, the paper is more readily grasped. Mounted AW there is less space for the fingers to acquire the paper. This is particularly true if the paper is torn off at the tangent of the roll and there is no free end hanging down.

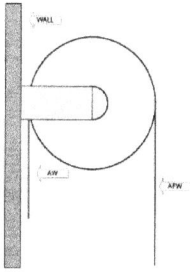

However, mounting the paper AW does make the paper obtrude into the room less, particularly as the paper is used up. For a cantilevered toilet paper holder, as the paper is used, the free end moves further away from the wall if the paper is mounted AW, and moves closer to the wall for AFW.

For printed paper an additional aesthetic component is introduced. Paper mounted AW will have the design hidden on that part of the paper extending off the roll.

Recessed into the wall - Examination of the recessed toilet

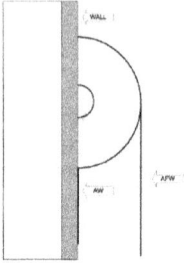

paper holder results in the same considerations as the cantilevered holder except that the approach to the paper is even more restricted when the paper is mounted AW. This form of mounting will place the loose end right against the wall,

regardless of how much of the paper has been used, making access more difficult. The closeness of the free end of the paper to the wall remains constant as the paper is used. The recessed toilet paper holder, when the paper is mounted AFW, places the free end sufficiently far from the wall for ease of access and yet closer to the wall than the cantilevered holder does. The free end of the paper moves closer to the wall as the paper roll decreases in size.

The aesthetics of the free end hanging down is the same as that for the cantilevered holder. Thus, for both the cantilevered holder and the recessed holder, for unprinted paper, the choice is between the aesthetic advantage of not having the loose end hanging into the room versus having the loose end of the paper more easily accessed.

In addition, for both the cantilevered holder and the recessed holder, for printed paper there is the question of the ease of accessibility and the choice of the two opposing aesthetic considerations. Since there is no method of quantifying aesthetics, the choice of mounting must be strictly personal. However, for printed paper, I may suggest that the aesthetics of viewing the printed surface of the hanging end and the convenience of accessing the loose end of the paper overweigh the negative aesthetics of the loose end hanging into the room. Thus, for printed paper the roll should be mounted in the AFW mode.

Hinged - For the hinged toilet paper hanger the analysis is

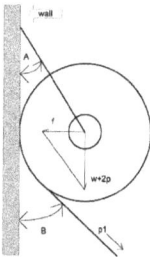

the same as for the recessed toilet paper. For paper rolls mounted AW, the difficulty of accessing the free end that is against the wall and remains against the wall as the paper is used is a major negative factor. An additional consideration for the hinged toilet paper hanger is the friction of the paper against the wall, which is not applicable in the other three mounting types.

For other than the hinged mount, the only friction involved is that of the roll on the roller and the roller in its support, and that is the same regardless of which direction the paper rolls. This friction against the wall may be desirable.   It may prevent accidentally pulling off more paper than is desired when trying to tear off a few sheets. The friction load of the paper against the wall is a function of many variables.   Those variables include the coefficient of friction between the wall surface and the paper (factors that go into the coefficient of friction are the wall surface, the paper surface, the ambient temperature, relative humidity, etc.), the weight of the paper roll plus that of the supporting rod, the angle of the hinged holder to the wall which, in turn, is a function of the amount of paper left on the roll, and the angle at which the paper is pulled from the roll.

All these factors are quantifiable, but extremely variable given that such things as wall surfaces are infinite in type and condition, paper textures are probably available in the hundreds, and support arm lengths vary from manufacturer to manufacturer. Therefore, I will address the matter of friction in general terms only.

Referring to the figures, w is the weight of the roll of toilet paper, its supporting rod, and a portion of the weight of the bracket. In a static condition there is a force, f, pressing the paper roll against the wall. f is w times the tangent of angle A. A is the angle formed by support bracket and the wall and is a function of the length of the support rod and the half diameter of the paper roll. The diameter of the paper roll is a function of the amount of paper remaining on the roll.

Starting with the paper mounted in the AFW position,

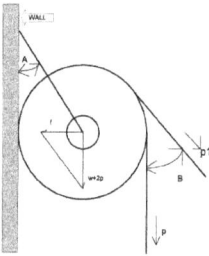

when the paper is pulled straight down with a force p, before the paper begins to roll there will be a force of 2p applied to center of the roll. This will add to the static force of w. Thus the force of the roll against the wall, f, will be (w+2p)tan A.

The starting friction is [(w+2p)tan A] times F (the coefficient of friction between the paper roll and the wall). The effort required to start the roll of toilet paper moving is the force, $p = (w \times \tan A \times F)/[1-(2 \times \tan A \times F)]$. With everything else held constant, the greater the angle A, the greater is the force, f, and thus the greater the pull, p, required to start the roll moving. Or to express it differently, it is easier to start an almost empty roll than a full role.

Of course, this analysis assumes that the paper is pulled straight down. If the paper is pulled with a force p1 at some angle from the vertical, B, the most usual situation, the force, f, will be less, $p1 = p - p \times \sin B$. Depending on the angle B, when the paper is pulled away from the wall the force, f, may equal zero and then there will be no starting friction (except for roller fiction).

When we take the AW mode of mounting the toilet paper

the situation is simplified. When the paper is pulled straight down, the only force that results in a starting friction is $f = w \times \tan A$, therefore $p = w \times \tan A \times F$. The pulling force for condition AW is significantly less than for condition AFW.

In addition, condition AW does not allow for a straight down pull on the toilet paper. The geometry of the human hand does not permit it. In all cases of condition AW the paper will be pulled at some angle, B, from the vertical. This angle will result in a force that is a function of the pulling force, p_1, in the horizontal direction opposite that of force f. The resultant force against the wall is $f = (w \times \tan A) - (p_1 \times \sin B)$. The pulling force required to start the roll moving is $p_1 = w \times F \times \tan A/(1 + \sin B)$. In all cases of angle B, the force against the wall resulting in starting friction, the pulling force of condition AW will be less than for condition AFW and will reach zero at a smaller angle B.

Thus, for the hinged toilet paper holder the choice is between the ease of accessing the paper in AFW versus the difficulty of grabbing the end of the toilet paper in AW; the aesthetics of having the paper against the wall and not seeing the printed side hanging down versus the aesthetics of seeing the printed side hanging down but obtruding into the room, (printed paper with words such as Thomas Crapper & Co.'s product would read upside down if mounted AW); plus having the additional force required to pull the paper off the roll in the AFW configuration.

One other factor should be considered for all methods of mounting toilet paper. I am told by cat owners that only the AW setting will do. If the paper is mounted AFW, the cat will quickly learn to pull down on the exposed portion of the toilet paper roll thus emptying the whole roll onto the floor. The choice is yours.

Chapter 9

EXCREMENT!

In my writings about toilets I purposely use several euphemisms for a four-letter word that most succinctly names the thing that is the center of interest of this book. There actually are only three words that I have used for the particular subject item. However, I do use the words as nouns, verbs, or modifiers in lieu of the forbidden word.

The three words in their various forms are:

1. *feces, feculence (n); fecal, feculent (a); to defecate (v).*

The *Oxford English Dictionary* (OED) traces the word, in at least one of its noun forms, to 1460, but the only use acknowledged is in the sense of sediment, dregs, lees, and refuse. It is easy to see how the current use of the word is derived from the dictionary definition. However, the OED does show some reticence in listing vulgar definitions of words. The verbal form of the word, using the prefix "de-" to indicate the removal of, is obvious.

Webster's New World Dictionary, 1970, does not show the same reluctance as the OED. In addition to a definition which parallels the OED definition, it defines "defecate" as "to excrete waste matter from the bowels." *Merriam-Webster's Collegiate Dictionary*, 1994, is a little more direct in its definition of "defecate": "to discharge feces from the bowels." But this is a circular definition.

2. *excreta, excrement (n); to excrete (v).*

The noun forms of this word are derived from the verb form *"ex,"* ("out") and *"cernere,"* which means "to sift or separate." The modern usage, particularly of the verbal form, often refers to matter other than feces. The word is found in the literature as far back as 1533.

3. *ordure (n).*

This word exists only in the noun form. It is defined in the OED as "filth, dirt" from the 12th century and as "excrement, dung" from 1388. Neither Menken nor Fowler include any of these words in their works. There are other polite words that have specific meanings, but are not usually used in reference to the human product and therefore I do not consider them to be appropriate for my use in my writings.

"Dung" is such a word. Along with "manure," the word usually describes the excreta of animals; however, on rare occasion, "dung" is used for the human product whereas "manure" is not.

"Coprolite" (κοπρος = dung + λιθος = stone) is another such word. This one, so beloved of paleontologists, is a special form of our subject matter, but not suitable for my use in the present tense. Two other words that are commonly used belong to the medical field. They are "bowel movement" and "stool." Although they are acceptable as polite euphemisms, they are usually limited to conversations with medical personnel and not considered refined enough for normal conversation, although it would be hard to find any subject of normal "polite" conversation where the banned word or its euphemisms would be needed.

I also do not use the word "crap" because I feel that it is considered by most people as being too coarse a word for serious writing or conversation. However, I have covered the origins of that word and its derivative "crapper" in another chapter, Naming the Unnamable, where I suggest that it is the best possible word for its use.

I also do not use children's words: "ca ca," "poo poo," or others of that ilk.

Chapter 10

A LAVATORY IS A PLACE TO WASH

In other chapters I have discussed such excruciatingly important subjects such as the name of a private room, the positioning of toilet seats, who was Crapper, the difference between Oriental and Occidental toilets, the position of females when urinating, the various terms for excrement, and how to hang toilet paper.

Now I am going to get even more personal. Those of you who prefer not follow me on this journey should read no further.

We are being exhorted more and more to wash our hands after using the toilet. Even so, a 1996 a survey found that only 60% of the people using the public toilets in Pennsylvania Station and Grand Central Station in New York washed their hands afterwards. Two years ago the survey was repeated. The percentage went down to 49.

The American Society for Microbiology and other groups have campaigned for us to wash our hands. At first it was only a mild admonition, then it became signs in restaurants directing employees. After that signs appeared in other public toilets for everyone. Electronic devices appeared to monitor conformance with directives (*Information Week*, May 25, 1998). No doubt, soon there will be laws mandating the practice.

This chapter is addressed to men because it is the only first-hand experience that I have. Why all this hype and pressure? Is a man's penis dirtier than other parts of his body? Let's examine the facts and see where it leads us.

Let's take you as a typical American male. You wake in the morning, use the toilet, and take a shower. At that point in time all parts of your body are equally clean. You dress, pick up the newspaper from the lawn in front of the house where who knows how many dogs have urinated and defecated, and have breakfast.

You get into your car and on your way to work you get some gas using the same hose that everyone else has used and then give your credit card to a clerk. He handles your card with his bare hands the same way that he has handled the cards of a dozen customers before you. You enter your office by turning the handle of the door which has been touched by every employee that preceded you to your office. You probably shake hands with several of your coworkers as you enter. Before starting work you decide to urinate.

So, off to the office men's room you go. There you either push open the door with your hand or turn a knob to get in. Then what do you do? If you are like most men, you belly up to the urinal, unzip your trousers, pull out your penis, and do what you must do. Then you put your penis back, zip up your trousers, and on your way out you see a sign suggesting that you wash your hands before returning to work. As a conscientious employee you do.

Whoops! What's wrong here? Has your penis, which has been under your clothing since you took your shower this morning, somehow soiled your hands which have been everywhere and touched everything? How did your penis manage to dirty your hands? Unless you urinated on your hands, which I most emphatically doubt you did. Even if you did (and that is a subject for another essay), there was no transfer of dirt from your penis to your hands, but rather from your hands to your penis.

Then why are you told to wash your hands after you urinated but not before? The outside of your penis is no more laden with bacteria and viruses than the rest of the skin on your body. In fact, under the described scenario, less so.

But your penis is "dirty," people will say. Is that true? "Dirty" has at least two meanings. It is obvious from the above scenario that your penis is cleaner (in sense of contamination) than your hands. But since most Americans are imbued with the Victorian concept that sex is "dirty" then it follows that any part of the body that is directly involved in the sex act is "dirty" and, like Lady Macbeth's hands, can never be washed clean. The moral "dirty" has been transformed into the unsanitary. Thus we are admonished to wash our hands after touching our "dirty" penises.

A Corollary

As noted above, most people shower in the morning. This practice is depicted on TV shows, in movies, and, of course, in advertisements. It is part of the American culture for cleanliness. Seldom is any mention made of showering in the evening. Yet cleanliness would be enhanced by showering in the evening rather than the morning. By showering in the morning rather than in the evening, a day's accumulation of dirt, dust, and detritus is brought to the bed the night before. The bed linens and bed clothing are dirtied. By showering at night, we'd go to bed clean and wake up clean, unless you sleep in a mud wallow.

My comments about washing hands before or after urinating can be extended to cover showering as well. Because the bed is the place where sex most often occurs, and sex is considered by many as morally dirty, and we as a society value moral cleanliness more than material cleanliness, we shower after rising rather than before going to bed.

Since most of us sleep with another person in bed with us, whether you feel that sex is morally dirty or not, whether you have sex or not, you are physically closer to that other person than to any other person at any other time. It seems to me that it is the height of inconsideration for a person not to shower before going to bed, and if we do, why then shower in the morning?

Chapter 11

WOMEN'S UNDERWEAR

I can claim some academic education and expertise on the subject of toilets, as I am a graduate and licensed engineer. In my professional career I have designed hundreds of toilet facilities in the U. S. and abroad. My interest in the non-technical aspects of toilets and related matters was initiated by my vocation and the necessity of learning about toilet matters in this and other cultures when designing toilets at home and overseas.

Now I am going to delve into a subject for which I claim no academic background or special knowledge —women's underwear, but this is also a logical consequence. In my general research on matters toilet I came across several references that indicated that until the 19th century most women in the Western world did not wear underwear.

For this tract we first must define "underwear." In the

broadest terms, "underwear" is anything worn under the outer garments, which for some writers includes petticoats, slips, shifts, girdles, blouses, perhaps even sweaters. For the purpose of this article I am restricting the word "underwear" to that subset of clothing encompassed in the broad term to those articles of clothing worn next to the body that also go between a woman's legs. In other words, an article of clothing that covers her genitals.

It became apparent that my sources, in saying that women did not wear underwear until recently, reference was being made to Western culture only, primarily Germany, France, England, and the United States. Prior to the middle of the 19th century women in those countries and other countries of similar cultures wore plenty of skirts and petticoats, but usually nothing underneath.

Even earlier, in the Middle Ages, the prevailing costume was a wrap-around tunic, but again, nothing underneath. The reasons that most women abjured the use of trousers or other close-fitting garments was the ever-present threat of crab lice and yeast infections (thrush). In those unsanitary and generally unwashed days, the enclosing of a warm and moist area would encourage the growth of both.

Also, before the advent of cotton and modern synthetic fabrics, consider how uncomfortable it would be with wool (think of the itchy bathing suits before the advent of synthetic fibers) or coarse linen underwear as compared to the airy coolness of nothing. Silk was available but very expensive and thus not used by the majority of the population.

In the Middle East, women did wear loose-fitting trousers, which, when they were introduced into Europe became known as drawers, because before the advent of rubber elastic, the trousers were held in place by a drawstring around the waist. Also, women in the Middle East and southern Europe bathed more often than their northern compatriots and didn't need to wear such heavy outer clothing because of the milder climate. There are ancient Roman mosaics depicting women dressed in what would best be described as bikinis, but this did not extend to northern Europe.

Of course, the lack of an undergarment had one other advantage before the coming of flush toilets. A woman could urinate and defecate almost anywhere as readily as a man and did. Any ditch or alleyway would do. And in those lustier times, a woman could accommodate her husband or lover with ease and dispatch. In opposition to that, rape was also easier. As noted in the police report of one of Jack the Ripper's victims in the late 19th century, the victim was not wearing drawers as would befit her supposed profession of prostitute.

Camargo, who became the greatest French ballet dancer in the mid-18th century, who shortened the traditional ballet skirt to the length that it is today, also introduced the *entrechat à quatre* (the movement in which the dancer jumps in the air and crosses her feet twice before coming down). This movement and the shorter skirt that she wore required her to wear a garment that preceded the general introduction of drawers by about a hundred years.

By the middle of the 19th century improvements in sanitation, personal hygiene, the breaking of the rubber monopoly in Brazil, and the bicycle all contributed to the increased use of women's underwear. Improved sanitation made it less necessary for women to urinate in public areas without toilet facilities.

Toilets, both public and private, became common.

Personal hygiene was advanced by the bringing of running water into the home so that women could cleanse themselves more easily. The breaking of the rubber monopoly allowed for cheap elastics, which removed the need for the use of drawstrings for under trousers. Drawstrings were uncomfortable and had a tendency to come undone at the most inopportune times, such as during a tennis match.

The bicycle became fashionable, even a fad, at the turn of the 20th century, necessitating a woman's garment that would allow her to sit astride the vehicle. That garment was the Bloomer. Amelia Jenks Bloomer did not invent the eponymous garment. That was done by Elizabeth Smith Miller.   Bloomer did popularize it starting in 1850. Originally it was loose ankle-length trousers under a knee-length skirt.

Since then women's skirts have gotten both shorter and longer, but the trouser (underpants) part has become shorter, tighter, and skimpier until today, for many women, it is hardly more than a string and a triangular piece of cloth, or what the French would call a *cache-sexe*.

For comparisons, we can look at other countries and cultures. In Japan, the kimono traditionally is worn with nothing underneath, as is the burnoose in Morocco, and similar garments in the Arab world. There is the story told in Japan that in a previous century, when all women wore the kimono, there was a fire in a two-story building. Several women refused to jump from the windows because they thought that their kimonos could be blown upwards and they would be exposed. They were burned in the fire.

Among men's clothing with skirts, Scottish kilt wearers do not traditionally wear any underwear, whereas Greek Evzones, who also wear skirts, wear what could be called white cotton pantyhose.

Which brings me to a conjecture. In the late eighteenth century, a law was promulgated in France that "no actress or dancer should appear on stage without drawers" which indicated that the general female population did not wear drawers. Laws are not written to prohibit an action which is not usually done. One century after the law was passed, the Can-Can as danced at the Moulin Rouge was considered to be scandalous and caused a sensation in Paris. Was it because the dancers were truly following the law when at the finale, they would turn away from the audience, bend over, and flip up their skirts?

Chapter 12

MUSLIMS

In the western world we assume that the normal position for a male urinating is upright, that is, standing. The majority of men in the western world do that. But in the Muslim world, which covers much of the Earth, that is not so. Islamic *sharee'ah* (the code of law based on the Koran) includes a number of rules and etiquettes to be followed when answering the call of nature.

What follows is an explanation of some of the rules governing urinating from a Muslim source. The source also provides extensive explanations of the laws regarding defecation. Rather than paraphrase the religious rulings, I present them as written. I have edited them for simplicity and clarity, but retained the language as written.

Not to face the *Qiblah* (direction of prayer, i.e. the Kabala) when urinating. This is out of respect for the *Qiblah* and for the symbols and rituals of Allah.

He should not touch his penis with his right hand when urinating, because the Prophet said, "When any one of you urinates, he should not hold his penis in his right hand or clean it with his right hand."

The Sunnah is to answer the call of nature sitting, making oneself close to the ground, because this is more concealing, and makes it less likely that spray from one's urine will come back on one's body or clothes, making them dirty. If a person can be sure of avoiding this, then it is permissible to urinate standing up.

A person should be concealed from the sight of others when answering the call of nature. If a person is out in an open space and cannot find anything to conceal him when he needs to answer the call of nature, he should move far away from the other people around him. A person should not uncover his *'awrah* (private parts) until after he has squatted close to the ground, because this is more concealing.

If a person is in a (modern) toilet, he should not lift his garment until he has closed the door and is out of sight of other people. With regard to this point and the one before, it is worth noting that the habit of many people in the West and elsewhere, of urinating in a standing position in front of other people in public toilets (using urinals) is something which goes against good manners, modesty and decency, and is repulsive to anyone who possesses sound common sense and wisdom.   How can anybody uncover in front of other people the *'awrah* (private parts) which Allah has placed between his legs to conceal it and commanded him to cover?

The idea that it should be covered is well established among all wise and decent people of all races. It is wrong in principle to build restrooms of this shameful type where the users can see one another, thus making them worse than some kinds of animals whose habit is to conceal themselves from one another when urinating or defecating.

He should be careful to remove all impurity after answering the call of nature, because the Prophet warned against being careless in cleaning oneself after urinating: "Most of the punishment of the grave will be because of urine." Ibn 'Abbaas reported that the Messenger of Allah passed by two graves, and said, "They are being punished, but they are not being punished for any major sin. One of them used not to protect himself (i.e. keep himself clean from) his urine, and the other used to walk about spreading malicious gossip."

The requirement for men to squat or sit while urinating may have begun with Mohammed, but the custom existed long before his time. I quote from a note in Richard Burton's translation of *A Thousand Nights and a Night* (1865). "In the East women stand on minor occasions while the men squat on their hunkers in a way hardly possible to an untrained European." Burton further quotes Herodotus about Arabia, who wrote in the fifth century B. C., "The women stand up when they make water, but the men sit down."

I can vouch that the second part of Herodotus' statement is still valid. This practice was strongly brought to my attention when I was in charge of designing the Saudi-Arabian Air Force Academy at Al-Kharj. There are no urinals in this all-male institution. We were directed by the Saudi liaison not to put any in the academy and the toilets could not face Mecca.

Chapter 13

RECENT DEVELOPMENTS

The waterless urinal uses no water for flushing. A trap with a chemical layer floating on top prevents sewer gases from coming up through the urinal. This fixture achieves the ultimate in water savings. The fixture, it is claimed, can pay for itself in a year by savings on utility bills.

On board cruise ships such as the Queen Elizabeth 2, where fresh water must be generated from seawater by distillation, the waterless toilet is installed in all public men's rooms.

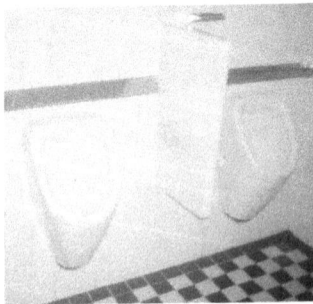

It shows up in many other places, especially those of high usage such as London's Heathrow Airport, Miami Pro Player Stadium, and Quality Inn International hotel in Orlando.

Among other innovations sold or actually put in service are self-cleaning toilet seats that after use rotate though a sanitizing and scented spray. In the Miami Airport a slightly different method of providing a sanitary seat is used. The seats are wrapped in plastic that changes at the push of a button.

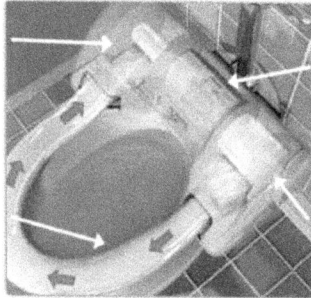

There are several devices on the market that convert an ordinary commode to a bidet. One type provides a water spray device under the seat. Another has a small basin that is moved over the opening when needed.

In Hollywood, ten animatronic toilets were made to be used in a film to warn pre-school age children of the dangers of an open toilet. In the film the toilet is shown to be alive and dangerous. It is shown to be eating little children, small animals, and toys. The purpose was to deter little children from playing in the toilet and possibly drowning. The actual result of test showings so traumatized the children that they could not use the toilet for its intended purpose without extensive therapy.

Microsoft has proposed an "iloo." This looks and operates similarly to a self-contained public toilet. In addition to the usual amenities, the iloo has a wireless keyboard, a flat screen monitor, and wireless LAN broadband connection. No mention is made of a printer, but that could be incorporated into the toilet paper dispenser so that secret messages could be disposed of.

ABOUT THE AUTHOR

Arthur Belefant is the author of several books and numerous magazine articles. Except for one published short story, all his writing is non-fiction. He was first published in the *Asahi Evening News* of Tokyo, Japan where he wrote a regular column, "The Gourmet's Guide" as a restaurant reviewer and food commentator for American expatriates in Japan.

He continued "The Gourmet's Guide" column when he moved back to the U.S. in the Melbourne, Florida publication *SCAM* for the Space Coast area Mensa group. For over ten years he covered such diverse subjects as food, Frankenstein, toilets, language, and politics.

He has also been published in several national magazines on technical and travel themes. A registered professional mechanical/electrical engineer, he has been hired to design buildings all over the world. Every building must have a toilet or two and so he has studied toilet design in many cultures across the globe.

www.ingramcontent.com/pod-product-compliance
Lightning Source LLC
LaVergne TN
LVHW051421080426
835508LV00022B/3182